The Layman's Articles of Confederation

Timothy Imholt Ph.D.

Michael Garst B.S.

The text used for the original sections of The Constitution of the United States was obtained from the National Archives. Their website can be found at:

www.archives.gov/exhibits/charters/charters_of_freedom_4.html

ISBN: 978-14997955806

ISBN-13: 1499795807

TIM'S DEDICATION

This book, like all my others, is dedicated to my late father, Louis Walter Imholt. He loved every aspect of this country's founding and was a true patriot. He also had no place for people 'lawyering' things as much as seems to happen currently. He also had very little patience for the modern crop of politicians. This book is a logical, understandable explanation of the US Constitution, what it means, and hopefully that can be achieved in such a way no one can guess my personal politics. I shall do my best Dad, I hope that this lives up to the standards you set for unbiased pursuit of facts.

MICHAEL'S DEDICTION

I want to dedicate this to my wonderful wife and kids for supporting me in this endeavor. Their steadfast support and acceptance made this possible for me and for that I am truly grateful. I would also like to dedicate to all the people who have made this country what it is, both good and bad, in the hopes of providing everyone the best chance they can to succeed. And lastly, I wish to thank my fellow author Tim for keeping me humble and giving me the chance.

CONTENTS

Introduction

Typically the books written concerning the documents that formed this Country are deep in either political viewpoints or "lawyerspeak." This book, as well as our previous work on the U.S. Constitution, represents our very best attempt to avoid those. In fact, it is our greatest hope that you will finish, having read this book, not being able to guess which political party we typically associate ourselves with, or if we associate with one at all. In reality, the more either of us listens to various elected officials from the two major political parties speak, the more we want to start a new one called "Common Sense," or perhaps "None of the Above."

This book came to be as a result of our previous publication on the U.S. Constitution. We wrote that book for many reasons, but after doing all the research to understand that document we wanted to dive into this other, less well understood, and certainly less widely read founding document.

Both of these books led us to believe that the various experts that show up on political radio talk shows or on the nightly television news may not have even read these documents much less made an honest attempt to understand them.

Some of these so-called experts sure do like to quote these documents with a far less than full understanding of them. In some cases the quotes provided are very...distant in their reflection of the actual words on the page.

We live in a Country where certain people like to misquote the Constitution on a regular basis and give little to no thought of where that document found its origins. It did not just appear as if from air. It came to be as a result, we believe, of this document. The Articles of Confederation was really, in our opinion, a rough draft for the Constitution we live under today.

So, since you are reading this you may be wondering...Who are these guys?

We are both enlisted Army Veterans, and more importantly, we are American's who care about the future of everyone who lives in this country. We don't just care about those who agree with us. We don't just care about those who vote along the same party lines as us, if we vote along a party line.

We care about all who proudly call themselves Citizens of these United States.

Throughout this book we will offer the exact text, as it was written, of the passage we are discussing. Next we will update the language into a more modern vernacular while attempting no disrespect to those who wrote the document.

We prefer to stand on the shoulders of giants rather than pretend to be giants ourselves.

This method is employed to make the document more understandable by modern day Americans. The original language uses many terms that are simply no longer used today. Between us, we, the former Enlisted Soldiers who wrote this book, we have three College Degrees. Each of us has a 4-year BS degree and one of us has PhD.

Finally, in each chapter, we will briefly attempt to explain what the words mean to us in an apolitical fashion.

We appreciate you giving us your time, and we hope we have honored those who gave us this Nation. Our only hope is that people will read this book and gain a better understanding of a Document that we should all understand, but not everyone has the time to take a semester (or two) long University Course.

We will try to divide this book up into digestible chunks consumable in a single sitting. Most of all, we hope that everyone who reads this will think about these words and the Founders who fought a War, while living under this document, to give us the Country we all love.

We hope you learn as much from reading this book as we learned by writing it.

Chapter 1

Introduction and Article I

Original Text to the Introduction and Article I of the Articles of Confederation

Introduction: To all to whom these Presents shall come, we, the undersigned Delegates of the States affixed to our Names send greeting. Whereas the Delegates of the United States of America in Congress assembled did on the fifteenth day of November in the year of our Lord One Thousand Seven Hundred and Seventy seven, and in the Second Year of the Independence of America agree to certain articles of Confederation and perpetual Union between the States of New Hampshire, Massachusetts-bay, Rhode Island and Providence Plantations, Connecticut, New York, New Jersey, Pennsylvania, Delaware, Maryland, Virginia, North Carolina, South Carolina, and Georgia in the Words following, viz. "Articles of Confederation and perpetual Union between the States of New Hampshire, Massachusetts-bay, Rhode Island and Providence Plantations, Connecticut, New York, New Jersey, Pennsylvania, Delaware, Maryland, Virginia,

North Carolina, South Carolina, and Georgia.

Article I. The Stile of this confederacy shall be, "The United States of America."

Modern Text to the Introduction and Article I of the Articles of Confederation

Introduction: To all those who read this document, we, the signers who are all delegates of the various States send greetings. This is done while the representatives of the United States of America assembled on the fifteenth day of November in the year of our Lord one thousand seven hundred and seventy seven. This was in the second year of the Independent American State and we agree upon these Articles of Confederation.

These Articles will ensure a perpetual union between the States of New Hampshire, Massachusetts Bay, Rhode Island and Providence Plantations, Connecticut, New York, New Jersey, Pennsylvania, Delaware, Maryland, Virginia, North Carolina, South Carolina and Georgia. This document represents those agreed upon Articles and will be the governing principals of this Nation.

Article I: The name of this confederacy shall be, "The United States of America."

Discussion

The Articles were this Nation's first set of federal

laws. It was intended to bind together the various colonies to accomplish, through responsible government, those things that no one State could do on its own. It was also intended to fix some issues that could (and had) arise in the areas of commerce, judicial jurisdiction and other minor governmental affairs.

It seems obvious the founders wrote this introduction and first article to just setup things that were about to be written into the document, and to give us an official name as a nation. They wanted the date, which colonies were involved, and the most interesting bit, they wanted to be sure that everyone understood this union was intended to be perpetual.

This government wasn't intended to be a temporary thing (as it turned out to be in the end, at least under this document), this Union of States was something they wanted to see continue forever.

This great Nation has, for the most part, survived…at least so far. We did break apart just a wee little bit during the Civil War, but in short order, the Union of States (which had grown from the original thirteen to thirty four by that point) was reassembled back into the United States of America. By the time the Civil War happened this document was no longer in effect and we were living under the Constitution we have now, but the ideal of the original union and the union itself has survived. That fact in itself is an astounding fact. These men were forming a very new type of government. It was a wild experiment, and it worked better than any of them probably expected once all the kinks were ironed out in the Constitution we have today.

The basic ideals that are in the Articles of Confederation really form the basis of the Constitution.

This, the Articles of Confederation, was essentially the rough draft for the document we have today. That will become far more obvious as we go through the Articles one by one.

Chapter 2

Article II

Original Text to Article II of the Articles of Confederation

Each state retains its sovereignty, freedom and independence, and every Power, Jurisdiction and right, which is not by this confederation expressly delegated to the United States, in Congress assembled.

Modern Text to Article II of the Articles of Confederation

Each state will retain its own sovereignty, freedom, and independence. The independent States retain every power, jurisdiction and right, which is not expressly delegated to the United States.

Discussion

The men, who were to become what we consider as our founding fathers, wrote this document while still in the middle of the Revolutionary War. The Articles of Confederation went into effect from 1781 until 1788, and considering the Revolutionary War did not end until 1783 some overlap between these two events can be seen.

The Articles, as a form of government, did not last too terribly long as there were some real issues with this structure that served to inhibit efficient government. The issues will become more apparent as these discussions continue.

This article is very brief, and basically just says that whatever is expressly not written as a power or responsibility of the federal government is a power left to the States. As we will see, they did not leave a lot of power in the hands of the federal government.

It appears that the founders wanted to be sure to have absolutely no chance of a large, heavy handed, over reaching federal government (like we have, in some ways, today).

These men really wanted to make sure there was as little power as possible in the form of a central authority. They probably drew this desire from the fact that they were still in the middle of a bitter fight to throw off a monarchy. That monarchy had become overly abusive in some of the laws and actions that were taken involving the colonies.

Could it be possible that more and more centralized power goes contrary to the ideas that founded this country?

That is possible.

No matter which side of the political spectrum

you consider yourself on, you must honestly admit that the size and power of the federal government has grown over the past few decades.

Does it matter?

These are questions we should ask ourselves.

These questions also represent some of the reasons that we should all strive to understand the documents that formed this great country. Absolutely all of the answers we seek are right there on the pages for all of us to read, and at the very least, be familiar with.

All we should to do is think for ourselves and attempt to apply these founding principles to our daily lives.

Congratulations for being someone who wants to understand these things better. We applaud you for your desire to learn about how the founding fathers wanted things to be done.

Chapter 3

Article III

Original Text to Article III of the Articles of Confederation

The said states hereby severally enter into a firm league of friendship with each other, for their common defence, the security of their Liberties, and their mutual and general welfare, binding themselves to assist each other, against all force offered to, or attacks made upon them, or any of them, on account of religion, sovereignty, trade, or any other pretence whatever.

Modern Text to Article III of the Articles of Confederation

The several States are hereby entered into a firm alliance of friendship with one another. This will allow them to provide for their common defense, secure their liberties, and provide for the mutual and general welfare. This alliance binds them together to assist one another against external force or attacks made on their territories. This is no matter if those attacks are made on account of religion, sovereignty, trade, or any other reasons whatsoever.

Discussion

One thing we noticed when reading this is that the article never identifies the United States as nation or kingdom. In fact, the entire document never once says that the United States is a nation in any form whatsoever. It only says that these various States are friends.

The States are entering into a formal union of some loose association. In essence, each state is its own nation, much like in the times of Ancient Greece.

The article does outline the purpose of this loosely affiliated States. In fact, the confederation has a very few things it exists to do. Those things are enumerated here and are common defense, secure various liberties and provide for the mutual defense as well as the general welfare.

This very short article goes one step further on the subject of common defense. The union of states will help one another if they are ever attacked from an external force (for instance another nation like…say…England).

It says that it doesn't matter why these attacks occur. Is it an attack for territory? Religion? Sovereignty? It doesn't matter according to this. If there is a threat or invasion, the States will pull their resources and defend themselves and their friends.

This is a common theme in the American culture, helping each other against threats. We know very few people that if their neighbor's house were being attacked, for whatever reason, that they would not lend a hand of some kind. No matter if that help was dialing 9-1-1 or whatever form it takes on, we tend to help one another. That was written into our earliest founding principles, and we hope it stays in our culture until the end of time. We feel this is one of the greatest traits about our nation.

Chapter 4

Article IV

Original Text to Article IV of the Articles of Confederation

The better to secure and perpetuate mutual friendship and intercourse among the people of the different states in this union, the free inhabitants of each of these states, paupers, vagabonds and fugitives from Justice excepted, shall be entitled to all privileges and immunities of free citizens in the several states; and the people of each state shall have free ingress and regress to and from any other state, and shall enjoy therein all the privileges of trade and commerce, subject to the same duties, impositions and restrictions as the inhabitants thereof respectively, provided that such restrictions shall not extend so far as to prevent the removal of property imported into any state, to any other State of which the Owner is an inhabitant; provided also that no imposition, duties or restriction shall be laid by any state, on the property of the united states, or either of them.

If any Person guilty of, or charged with, treason,

felony, or other high misdemeanor in any state, shall flee from Justice, and be found in any of the united states, he shall upon demand of the Governor or executive power of the state from which he fled, be delivered up, and removed to the state having jurisdiction of his offence.

Full faith and credit shall be given in each of these states to the records, acts and judicial proceedings of the courts and magistrates of every other state.

Modern Text to Article IV of the Articles of Confederation

To better ensure and perpetuate the mutual friendship as well as interaction among the people of the various States in the union, the free inhabitants of each State, with the exception of fugitives from justice, shall be entitled to all privileges and immunities of free citizens. The people of each State shall have free entry and return to, and from, any other State. The citizens of each State shall enjoy all the privileges of trade and commerce subject to the same duties, obligations, and restrictions of residents of each respective State, provided that such restrictions do not prevent the removal of property important to any State of which the owner is a resident. No State shall place an obligation, duty or restriction on the property of the United States or any of the other States of this union.

If a person is guilty of, or charged with, treason, felony, or other high misdemeanor in any State, then flees from justice, and is found to be in any of the other States of this Union, they shall be returned to the State in which the offense took place upon request of the Governor or executive of that original State.

Records, acts, and judicial proceedings of the courts and judges considered valid in one State shall be considered valid, as well as given full faith and credit, in every other State.

Discussion

This article is where we start to see more meat on the bones, so to speak, of this document. It does a few things to start to provide a framework for the citizenry of the several States as far as rights are concerned.

The first thing is the travel in between States issue. Because the Articles of Confederation didn't really set up one nation, it set up a loosely affiliated group of member States there were probably going to be very different laws in different States.

Let's say, for the sake of argument, that there was some right in New York that they didn't have in New Jersey. Someone travels from New Jersey into New York; therefore they now enjoy that privilege. This does go both ways. Now let's assume that the reverse travel direction is true. New Yorkers are not free from the laws of New Jersey if they are more restrictive. When you are in a State you are bound by the laws, or lack thereof, in the State you are currently occupying. That way you couldn't just walk into New Jersey and say something like "but murder is legal in New York."

This article also did another thing regarding travel between States. It says that if you are from Pennsylvania and you *want* to go to New York (or any other combination of States); you are free to do so. You do not need special permission; you don't need (in a modern sense) a passport. You could freely travel from any State, to any State that you want, just make sure you are home (or at your destination) in time for dinner (or for your mother to call and check on you).

It is in this article we also start to cover what happens in various cases involving the judicial system. It says that if there is a fugitive from justice that quickly runs out of one State where they are wanted for some crime and into another State it is required that whatever State the fugitive, provided he can be located, is in, hands him over to where he is accused of the crime, so that he may stand trial. This is not a bad thing to ensure. Otherwise crime sprees would very likely sprout up right around the border of every State so that criminals could just run a short distance to somewhere they couldn't be found guilty.

The final thing this article does was carried over (as was much of this article) into the Constitution that we have today. It says, very specifically, that full faith and credit will be given to the records and acts of one of the several States by every other State. Even the wording used here is virtually identical to what was put in the Constitution after the Articles were abandoned, and in the Constitutional sense usually referred to as the full faith and credit clause.

Basically what this full faith and credit clause does is to say that if you are licensed in one State to do something, for instance drive, you are licensed in every other State. Now, we know the founders didn't have cars or drivers licenses but this is in the modern sense. They had their equivalents of the day.

One thing neither of us can figure out, and we someday hope that either the news media or the Supreme Court (is there really a difference anymore?) sorts out, is the issue of marriage. This full faith and credit section should apply in this case.

There are certain types of marriage allowed in some States that may not be recognized in other States. This is the subject of heated argument of the day for some parts of the general population. If one State allows same sex marriage is that marriage recognized in every other State?

Now I know someone is going to argue and say it shouldn't be allowed in any State. This is one of the few times I can say I don't care. You can believe in same sex marriage or not but you have to ask yourself…Constitutionally (or Articles of Confederation) speaking can one State refuse to recognize a marriage that is allowed in another State?

Could the next type of marriage blocked be between men and women?

It is a slippery slope to start knowingly violating the Constitution and it seems clear that in this case there are some Constitutional (and would have been Article of Confederation issues) to sort out.

You can also ask yourself the same question about concealed carry permits for weapons. If you have a license in one State (Texas for instance) why does that permit not apply in New York? Another interesting Constitutional question that should be sorted out because according to the full faith and credit clause it seems logical that those permits should apply.

Chapter 5

Article V

Original Text to Article V of the Articles of Confederation

For the more convenient management of the general interests of the united states, delegates shall be annually appointed in such manner as the legislature of each state shall direct, to meet in Congress on the first Monday in November, in every year, with a power reserved to each state to recall its delegates, or any of them, at any time within the year, and to send others in their stead, for the remainder of the Year.

No State shall be represented in Congress by less than two, nor by more than seven Members; and no person shall be capable of being delegate for more than three years, in any term of six years; nor shall any person, being a delegate, be capable of holding any office under the united states, for which he, or another for his benefit receives any salary, fees or emolument of any kind.

Each State shall maintain its own delegates in a meeting of the states, and while they act as members of the committee of the states.

In determining questions in the United States, in Congress assembled, each state shall have one vote.

Freedom of speech and debate in Congress shall not be impeached or questioned in any Court, or place out of Congress, and the members of congress shall be protected in their persons from arrests and imprisonments, during the time of their going to and from, and attendance on congress, except for treason, felony, or breach of the peace.

Modern Text to Article V of the Articles of Confederation

In order to better manage the general interests of the United States, delegates shall be appointed on an annual basis in a method determined by the legislature of each State. These delegates will meet in Congress on the first Monday in November, every year. Each State reserves the power to recall some or all of its delegates at any time, for any reason, within the year. If a State recalls its delegates that State must send replacement delegates for the remainder of the year.

No State shall have less than two or more than seven members in the Congress at any one time. No person from a State elected to the Congress shall be a delegate for more than three years inside a six-year time period. No person who is a delegate will hold an office under the United States in which he or she, or someone else for his or her benefit, receives any kind of salary, fee or payment of any kind.

Each State shall pay for their own delegates while they are in a meeting of the States, and while they act as members of the Committee of the States.

In determining questions posed to the United States, in the assembled Congress, each State shall have one vote without regard to the number of delegates.

Freedom of speech and debate in Congress will not be prosecuted or questioned in any Court, or any other place outside of Congress. The members of Congress shall be protected from arrest or imprisonment while they are going to, from, or attending Congress with the exception of treason, felony, or breach of peace.

Discussion

Under the Articles of Confederation, just as we do under the Constitution, we had a Congress. The difference is that under these original founding laws the Congress was unicameral, or only one House. There was no Senate and House of Representatives; the Congress was one legislative body. In the original document it was always referred to as The United States in

Congress Assembled, which is a big fancy way of saying the Congress of the United States is having a meeting.

In order to send members to the Congress, there was not an election of the citizens of each State. No, no, no, not under these Articles of Confederation, that would have been way too easy.

The Legislatures of each State would choose their Congressional members and could send any number of them that particular State wanted to between two members and seven. These delegates could only serve three years out of every six, in other words they had term limits.

Now comes the catch. No matter how many delegates each State sent, when it came to voting each State would get one vote. In other words the States voted as States. The delegates from that State would have to get together and decide what their State would do before entering an official yes or no vote.

Is this a good way to do things?

Think about the last time you asked your significant other on what they wanted for dinner, and that is just the two of you. Now add in your in laws and parents and throw in a child as well, and ask the same question. Someone is going to go out to dinner with hurt feelings and very upset. Getting a consensus from any number of people greater than one, all of whom feel passionate about a topic can be rather, let just say, difficult.

We find another carry over into the Constitution within this article. It guarantees the freedom of speech in Congress (to Congressmen not to citizens). It basically says that all members of Congress are immune to prosecution for anything they say in meetings during the Congressional sessions.

It is interesting to us, and worth pointing out, that that this didn't apply outside of Congressional sessions. It did, however, also give members of Congress the right to be free from arrest when going from to and from Congressional meetings except in the matters of treason, felony or breach of peace.

It is kind of interesting that the rule makers were, at least in some small ways, making themselves immune to some of the very laws they were making for the citizens of the States. There is some of that being carried over in modern day.

Today these same attitudes are at play; however, interestingly there are other rules which modern day Congressmen and elected federal officials have exempted themselves from. One of the big ones is that they can profit on insider information.

That wasn't unheard of in the early days either. Some of the founding fathers may have gotten printing contracts (among other things) as a result of legislation they had a hand in crafting.

Let's get back to the modern day culmination of these things. The insider trading rules that apply to stock market transactions to every other citizen in the country do not apply to these federal officials today.

How does this happen?

Someone, let's just say a CEO that lives in the district of a particular Congressperson has some non-public information that will cause a stock to skyrocket. They are free to share that information with certain federal officials, although according to the SEC they are not to disclose that information publicly. Interestingly those officials are free to profit off of that information, yet the general public gets in on the deal too late to make the big profit margins.

Could that be how, at least in part, most of the people in Congress become very wealthy while in these offices?

Could that have been avoided had these exemptions not been written in from the earliest days?

Should lawmakers in any country ever be allowed to say that the laws they pass do not apply to themselves?

Should we need to pass a federal law that says exemptions to other laws are illegal?

The whole thing just seems odd from the get-go.

This particular bit was put into our founding documents as far back as The Articles of Confederation, and then carried over into the Constitution.

Perhaps...just maybe there should be a Constitutional amendment to change this rule of immunity that has been on the books from the earliest days of this country. We, the authors, may have to disagree with the founders on this one. All laws MUST apply to ALL citizens, not merely those outside of official office. We wonder if there is an earlier example of these sorts of exemptions written into law?

Perhaps if someone reading this knows of one you can contact us and let us know.

If the Congress decides that a particular law is in the best interest of the Citizens of the United States, then the members of Congress logically must abide by that new law. There are several examples of how Congress has not done that for anyone who cares to look for them. We suggest to each and every person, look into this, make your voice heard, and give Congress a big kick in the backside to start doing what is right for everyone including him or herself, not just selected individuals.   Don't let them lean on what was an obvious oversight of the founding fathers and use that to enrich themselves while in office. These offices should be a privilege not a pathway to becoming one of the wealthiest people in the world.

Chapter 6

Article VI

Original Text to Article VI of the Articles of Confederation

No State, without the Consent of the united States, in congress assembled, shall send any embassy to, or receive any embassy from, or enter into any conferrence, agreement, alliance, or treaty, with any King prince or state; nor shall any person holding any office of profit or trust under the united states, or any of them, accept of any present, emolument, office, or title of any kind whatever, from any king, prince, or foreign state; nor shall the united states, in congress assembled, or any of them, grant any title of nobility.

No two or more states shall enter into any treaty, confederation, or alliance whatever between them, without the consent of the united states, in congress assembled, specifying accurately the purposes for which the same is to be entered into, and how long it shall continue.

No State shall lay any imposts or duties, which may interfere with any stipulations in treaties, entered into by the united States in congress assembled, with any king, prince, or State, in pursuance of any treaties already proposed by congress, to the courts of France and Spain.

No vessels of war shall be kept up in time of peace, by any state, except such number only, as shall be deemed necessary by the united states, in congress assembled, for the defence of such state, or its trade; nor shall any body of forces be kept up, by any state, in time of peace, except such number only as, in the judgment of the united states, in congress assembled, shall be deemed requisite to garrison the forts necessary for the defence of such state; but every state shall always keep up a well regulated and disciplined militia, sufficiently armed and accounted, and shall provide and constantly have ready for use, in public stores, a due number of field pieces and tents, and a proper quantity of arms, ammunition, and camp equipage.

No State shall engage in any war without the consent of the united States in congress assembled, unless such State be actually invaded by enemies, or shall have received certain advice of a resolution being formed by some nation of Indians to invade such State, and the danger is so imminent as not to admit of a delay till the united states in congress assembled, can be consulted: nor shall any state grant commissions to any ships or vessels of war, nor letters of marque or reprisal, except it be after a declaration of war by the united states in congress assembled, and then only against the kingdom or State, and the subjects thereof, against which war has been so declared, and under such regulations as shall be established by the united states in congress assembled, unless such state be infested by pirates, in which case vessels of war may be fitted out for that occasion, and kept so long as the danger shall continue, or until the united states in congress assembled shall determine otherwise.

Modern Text to Article VI of the Articles of Confederation

No State, without the consent of the Congress of the United States, shall send a delegation to, receive a delegation from, or enter into a discussion, agreement, alliance, or treaty with any king, prince or foreign state. No person holding a salaried office or position of trust under the United States, or any of the States of the union, may accept any present, payment, office, or title of any kind from a king, prince, or foreign state.

The Congress of the United States will not grant any title of nobility.

No two or more States shall enter into a treaty, coalition, or alliance between themselves, without the consent of the Congress of the

United States. The States wishing to do so must accurately specify the purpose for which the proposed treaty, coalition, or alliance is being formed, and how long it is to continue.

No State shall put in place any taxes or duties, which may interfere with any of the stipulations in treaties to which the Congress of the United States has become a signatory. These include any treaties, existing or future, with a king, prince, or foreign state, including those already proposed by Congress to the courts of France and Spain.

No vessels intended for use in war shall be kept in time of peace, by any of the member States, except in such quantity as shall be deemed necessary by the Congress of the United States. This quantity will be the number deemed necessary for defense of the States and their trade. No group of forces shall be kept by any State in time of peace, except in the quantity judged necessary by the Congress of the United States to garrison the forts necessary for defensive purposes. Each State shall keep a well-regulated and disciplined militia, sufficiently armed. Each State shall provide and keep ready for use, in public storage, field equipment, tents, and a proper quantity of arms and ammunition to equip their militia.

No State shall engage in any war without the consent of the Congress of the United States unless that State has been invaded by enemy forces or unless that State has received a resolution being formed by some Nation of Indians to invade the State, and the danger is so imminent that delay of defense until the Congress of the United States can be assembled and consulted.

No State shall grant commissions to any ships or vessels of war, nor letters of reprisal, except after a declaration of war by the Congress of the United States. Once that declaration of war has been made, the States may only perform these tasks against the enemy that is the subject of the declaration of war. These will only be done by the States under regulations as shall be established by the Congress of the United States, unless the State is infested by pirates. In that case vessels of war may be fitted for the occasions, and kept only long as long as the danger exists, or until the Congress of the United States can assemble and determine otherwise.

Discussion

This entire section is, essentially, the limitations that are placed on the individual States. For instance, only the central government can establish formal relationships with other countries. The articles don't care if the relationship is political, commercial, or even a declaration of War, it is not something a State can do on its own under these laws. The federal system is to retain those particular functions.

It does, in the long run, make sense to have some functions that States should not do on their own. Imagine that chaos that could result if all of the States of the Union could decide different import rules and regulations, or even if there were different qualifications for Doctors. It would just be a mess.

There are times when State officials will meet with foreign leaders, that is still allowed. However, during those meetings no State or State official can accept gifts or titles (for instance nobility) from these foreign countries. They specifically call out Nobility, it appears the men who wrote this, while in the middle of what we now refer to as the Revolutionary War were attempting to be free of a monarchy, and were highly leery of anything that suggested nobility or Nobles.

If you examine their other writing they did not want to create any kind of noble class in the new Nation. That was the last thing any of them wanted to see. While we don't have an official King or Queen we do have certain families that come close (for example Bush, Kennedy, Clinton). However, we do have free elections and, at any point in time we are able to end that dynasty and get rid of those groups, which would not be true if we had an officially declared Noble class.

The part of this article about States entering into

alliances seemed a little strange at first. Then we thought more carefully about it, and it makes sense that this would be in here. If it was not, there is a chance that a small number of States, say three of them, could get together and make some kind of sub-country within a country. Perhaps three or four could band together and dictate votes to the remainder of the country.

Think about for a second, they had thirteen States (colonies). If seven of them formed a pact they could essentially dictate anything they wanted to the remainder of the States. While it could have very easily happened, the founders thought ahead and ensured it never would, at least not through some formal pact. In reality when Congress meets (even today) there are groups that will work together to achieve their goals but this is all done on a case-by-case basis not through some formal "you and I always vote together" agreement.

There were some other housekeeping issues in here involving taxes and treaties. Just some run of the mill stuff. But there is one thing that stands out in our minds.

No State could have, on its own, engaged in War, without the permission of the Congress. This makes sense, so that Massachusetts, for instance, couldn't decide to go to War with France and drag everyone else along with them. It has to be the decision of the majority of the

States.

The only exception to this is if a State has been invaded or is imminent danger of being invaded.

The other interesting line that reminds us just how different life was for these men is that a State may engage in War if infested by pirates. That's right…pirates. Think about that…pirates. As in Arrrr me matey, guys with a wooden peg legs and a parrot on their shoulder waving a cutlass around.

It also puts in writing that each State is required to maintain a well regulated, and well trained militia. They must keep these militia units equipped, with sufficient equipment in public storage, at, presumably, public expense. It even outlines what some of this equipment should be, arms, ammunition, tents, etc. All of these things are to provide for the common defense, but this is where they start to outline the details of how that common defense is going to be maintained.

These parts of the Articles of Confederation as well as their eventual carryovers into Constitution have become a hotly debated issue in today's society. As we have pointed out previously, we have been clear that we will not state our own beliefs on the Second Amendment of the Constitution.

What we will do is point out that the Articles of Confederation state specifically about a well maintained and armed militia as well as maintaining equipment meant for the protection of the general public such as tents, field arms (also known as artillery) and ammunition. While it does not mention what we currently classify as assault weapons, it did mean the military weapons of the day (which were their version of our Assault weapons) as they were one in the same between military and civilian grade weapons. Notice also that it specifies this thing about kept in storage but it doesn't specific in the hands of the general pubic. Now this language is different in our modern Constitution but this document was the foundation for that one and should be considered when talking about the original intent of the founders.

Today military grade weapons are much different than their civilian counterparts. The same cannot be said in the time period in which this was written, and that, perhaps, is where the real disagreements begin amongst those on both sides of this argument find their origin.

Chapter 7

Article VII

Original Text to Article VII of the Articles of Confederation

When land forces are raised by any state, for the common defence, all officers of or under the rank of colonel, shall be appointed by the legislature of each state respectively by whom such forces shall be raised, or in such manner as such state shall direct, and all vacancies shall be filled up by the state which first made appointment.

Modern Text to Article VII of the Articles of Confederation

When a land force (Army) is raised by any State in order to provide for the common defense, all officers under the rank of Colonel will be appointed by the legislature of that State. If the State writes a law that dictates a different method then it is that State's law which will determine the method by which these officers are appointed. All vacancies amongst the officer corps shall be filled by the State that first made the appointment. The Congress shall appoint officers with ranks higher than Colonel.

Discussion

This particular article is short, sweet and to the point. It basically says that when a military is raised for the common defense any officer under the rank of Colonel will be appointed by the legislature of the State fielding that officer. In order to promoted to higher rank (General in the Army, Admiral in the Navy) in a modern sense it takes an act of Congress, a tradition that finds its origin under the Articles of Confederation.

We were both enlisted soldiers. In order to be promoted in those ranks, in the modern military, it is a point system. You make the right number of points (for the most part, there are exception where someone with fewer points can be promoted) and you are promoted. While this is a very bland description of how enlisted get promoted (and there are many details we are leaving out) it is, we think, the best way of getting a promotion. It doesn't lend itself too much in the direction of politics. It is, essentially, a purely merit based method. Officers, on the other hand, are much different, and that tradition dates back to this original form of government, at least in this country.

We will spare you any more details in the process for Colonels and below, as it is strange enough, and could be the subject of an entire book.   Above Colonel, in the General (or Admiral for those Navy/Coastie type people) ranks it gets even stranger, and historically that comes from the Articles of Confederation (and prior in other countries). From these founding documents there is a caveat for Generals, which still carries through to today. If an officer is up for promotion to General it is up to the elected federal officeholders to add that officers name to the possible promotion list. Once that officer is on the list, it is then federal elected officials that confirm them for this promotion.

That is about as political as a promotion could ever be, and began here.

Again while this is a very general (no pun intended) view on how flag grade officers get promoted, the process has not really changed for the last 200+ years. The only difference in our recent past was that there were some flag ranked officers who were nothing but a political promotion and had never actually had to lead men (and now women) into battle.

In a modern sense, those prospective officers have to go through some pretty serious vetting (or friend making) to make sure they know their stuff, and have advocates to argue for their promotion.

We are both really glad we never had to go through such crap in our careers. It is probably a good thing for officers to have to be approved at the highest levels of our government but we both think we dodged a bullet by not having to cope with such a political claptrap.

Chapter 8

Article VIII

Original Text to Article VIII of the Articles of Confederation

All charges of war, and all other expenses that shall be incurred for the common defence or general welfare, and allowed by the united states in congress assembled, shall be defrayed out of a common treasury, which shall be supplied by the several states, in proportion to the value of all land within each state, granted to or surveyed for any Person, as such land and the buildings and improvements thereon shall be estimated, according to such mode as the united states, in congress assembled, shall, from time to time, direct and appoint. The taxes for paying that proportion shall be laid and levied by the authority and direction of the legislatures of the several states within the time agreed upon by the United States in congress assembled.

Modern Text to Article VIII of the Articles of Confederation

If the Congress of the United States directs costs as a result of war or other expenses resulting from the common defense or general welfare, these costs shall be paid from a common treasury. The treasury shall be supplied by the several States.

The portion of that treasury that comes from each State is in proportion to the value of all land within each State, with the value of buildings and improvements to be estimated. These values shall be determined in a method determined by the Congress of the United States. The taxes for paying that portion of the treasure that is the responsibility of each of the several States are due within the time agreed upon by the Congress of the United States.

Discussion

This article outlines how the treasury of the United States gets funding on deposit. Basically what they would have done is charged a property tax on all the States. It would have worked in much the same fashion as property taxes on an individual's home that get paid to the city and county in the more modern sense, only in this case the State would owe it to the federal government.

Something jumped out at us. The Congress gets to decide how a determination is made for the value of the land. That actually holds with today's property tax valuation methods. However, it doesn't set a date for when this is due. It merely says, essentially, the monies are due is at the discretion of and date determined by the Congress.

Does that mean it isn't every year?

Could it be only as needed?

These are questions that aren't covered in the document. They were left for later.

Who is responsible for doing the estimates of the values?

The Congress sets the method, but who actually does the estimation?

Is it the States?

If it is the States who do the estimation, on their own property values no less, is it possible they would estimate very low to prevent having to pay a high tax level?

Would they also not honestly represent the interests by saying they truly had less developed areas as well, minimizing what they have to pay in taxes as well?

All of these questions are left unanswered in a section that is really…very poorly written. Tax laws are most effective when they are specific, and this is a very loosely written section.

There is another thing that is left out, that might just become needed in the long run.

It never specifies any penalties if a State refuses to pay their taxes in a timely fashion.

What happens in the event one of the States refuses to meet the agreed upon deadline?

Is there a penalty?

Do they just get away with it?

This section is very lacking in any measure of needed specificity.

Chapter 9

Article IX

Original Text to Article IX of the Articles of Confederation

The United States, in congress assembled, shall have the sole and exclusive right and power of determining on peace and war, except in the cases mentioned in the sixth article - of sending and receiving ambassadors - entering into treaties and alliances, provided that no treaty of commerce shall be made, whereby the legislative power of the respective states shall be restrained from imposing such imposts and duties on foreigners, as their own people are subjected to, or from prohibiting the exportation or importation of any species of goods or commodities whatsoever - of establishing rules for deciding, in all cases, what captures on land or water shall be legal, and in what manner prizes taken by land or naval forces in the service of the united Sates, shall be divided or appropriated - of granting letters of marque and reprisal in times of peace - appointing courts for the trial of piracies and felonies committed on the high seas; and establishing courts; for receiving and determining finally appeals in all cases of captures; provided that no member of congress shall be appointed a judge of any of the said courts.

The united states, in congress assembled, shall also be the last resort on appeal, in all disputes and differences now subsisting, or that hereafter may arise between two or more states concerning boundary, jurisdiction, or any other cause whatever; which authority shall always be exercised in the manner following. Whenever the legislative or executive authority, or lawful agent of any state in controversy with another, shall present a petition to congress, stating the matter in question, and praying for a hearing, notice thereof shall be given, by order of congress, to the legislative or executive authority of the other state in controversy, and a day assigned for the appearance of the parties by their lawful agents, who shall then be directed to appoint, by joint consent, commissioners or judges to constitute a court for hearing and determining the matter in question: but if they cannot agree, congress shall name three persons out of each of the united states, and from the list of such persons each party shall alternately strike out one, the petitioners beginning, until the number shall be reduced to thirteen; and from that number not less than seven, nor more than nine names, as congress shall direct, shall, in the presence of congress, be drawn out by lot, and the persons whose names shall be so drawn, or any five of them, shall be commissioners or judges, to hear and finally determine the controversy, so always as a major part of the judges, who shall hear the cause, shall agree in the determination: and if either party shall neglect to attend at the day appointed, without showing reasons which congress shall judge sufficient, or being present, shall refuse to strike, the congress shall proceed to nominate three persons out of each State, and the secretary of congress shall strike in behalf of such party absent or refusing; and the judgment and sentence of the court, to be appointed in the manner before prescribed, shall be final and conclusive; and if any of the parties shall refuse to submit to the authority of such court, or to appear or defend their claim or cause, the court shall nevertheless proceed to pronounce sentence, or judgment, which shall in like manner be final and decisive; the judgment or sentence and other proceedings being in either case transmitted to congress, and lodged among the acts of congress, for the security of the parties concerned: provided that every commissioner, before he sits in judgment, shall take an oath to be administered by one of the judges of the supreme or superior court of the State where the cause shall be tried, "well and truly to hear and determine the matter in question, according to the best of his judgment, without favour, affection, or hope of reward: "provided, also, that no State shall be deprived of territory for the benefit of the united states.

All controversies concerning the private right of soil claimed under different grants of two or more states, whose jurisdictions as they may respect such lands, and the states which passed such grants are adjusted, the said grants or either of them being at the same time claimed to have originated antecedent to such settlement of jurisdiction, shall, on the petition of either party to the congress of the united states, be finally determined, as near as may be, in the same manner as is before prescribed for deciding disputes respecting territorial jurisdiction between different states.

The united states, in congress assembled, shall also have the sole and exclusive right and power of regulating the alloy and value of coin struck by their own authority, or by that of the respective states - fixing the standard of weights and measures throughout the united states - regulating the trade and managing all affairs with the Indians, not members of any of the states; provided that the legislative right of any state, within its own limits, be not infringed or violated - establishing and regulating post-offices from one state to another, throughout all the united states, and exacting such postage on the papers passing through the same, as may be requisite to defray the expenses of the said office - appointing all officers of the land forces in the service of the united States, excepting regimental officers - appointing all the officers of the naval forces, and commissioning all officers whatever in the service of the united states; making rules for the government and regulation of the said land and naval forces, and directing their operations.

The united States, in congress assembled, shall have authority to appoint a committee, to sit in the recess of congress, to be denominated, "A Committee of the States," and to consist of one delegate from each State; and to appoint such other committees and civil officers as may be necessary for managing the general affairs of the united states under their direction - to appoint one of their number to preside; provided that no person be allowed to serve in the office of president more than one year in any term of three years; to ascertain the necessary sums of money to be raised for the service of the united states, and to appropriate and apply the same for defraying the public expenses; to borrow money or emit bills on the credit of the united states, transmitting every half year to the respective states an account of the sums of money so borrowed or emitted, - to build and equip a navy - to agree upon the number of land forces, and to make requisitions from each state for its quota, in proportion to the number of white inhabitants in such state, which requisition shall be binding; and thereupon the legislature of each state shall appoint the regimental officers, raise the men, and clothe, arm, and equip them, in a soldier-like manner, at the expense of the united states; and the officers and men so clothed, armed, and equipped, shall march to the place appointed, and within the time agreed on by the united states, in congress assembled; but if the united states, in congress assembled, shall, on consideration of circumstances, judge proper that any state should not raise men, or should raise a smaller number than its quota, and that any other state should raise a greater number of men than the quota thereof, such extra number shall be raised, officered, clothed, armed, and equipped in the same manner as the quota of such state, unless the legislature of such state shall judge that such extra number cannot be safely spared out of the same, in which case they shall raise, officer, clothe, arm, and equip, as many of such extra number as they judge can be safely spared. And the officers and men so clothed, armed, and equipped, shall march to the place appointed, and within the time agreed on by the united states in congress assembled.

The united states, in congress assembled, shall never engage in a war, nor grant letters of marque and reprisal in time of peace, nor enter into any treaties or alliances, nor coin money, nor regulate the value thereof nor ascertain the sums and expenses necessary for the defence and welfare of the united states, or any of them, nor emit bills, nor borrow money on the credit of the united states, nor appropriate money, nor agree upon the number of vessels of war to be built or purchased, or the number of land or sea forces to be raised, nor appoint a commander in chief of the army or navy, unless nine states assent to the same, nor shall a question on any other point, except for adjourning from day to day, be determined, unless by the votes of a majority of the united states in congress assembled.

The congress of the united states shall have power to adjourn to any time within the year, and to any place within the united states, so that no period of adjournment be for a longer duration than the space of six Months, and shall publish the Journal of their proceedings monthly, except such parts thereof relating to treaties, alliances, or military operations, as in their judgment require secrecy; and the yeas and nays of the delegates of each State, on any question, shall be entered on the Journal, when it is desired by any delegate; and the delegates of a State, or any of them, at his or their request, shall be furnished with a transcript of the said

Journal, except such parts as are above excepted, to lay before the legislatures of the several states.

Modern Text to Article IX of the Articles of Confederation

The Congress of the United States shall have the sole and exclusive right and power of determining the following issues:

- Determining peace and war, except in those cases mentioned in the sixth article.
- Of sending and receiving ambassadors.
- Of entering into treaties and alliances, provided that no treaty of commerce shall be made. The legislative power of the several States shall be restrained from imposing taxes and duties on foreigners, as their own citizens are subjected to, or from prohibiting the exporting or importing of any type of goods or commodities whatsoever.
- The following issues involving legalities:
  - Of establishing rules for deciding, in all cases, which captures on land or water are legal, and in what way prizes are taking by land or naval forces in the services of the United States will be divided amongst the soldiers and sailors.
  - Of granting letters of marque and reprisal in peacetime.

- o Of appointing judges to courts for the trial of piracies and felonies committed on the high seas.
- o Of establishing courts.
- o For receiving and determining final appeals in all cases of captures.
- o No member of the Congress shall be appointed to be a judge of any of the courts or court related issues.

The Congress of the United States shall be the appeal of last resort, in all disputes and differences now subsisting, or that may arise after this date between two or more States concerning boundaries, jurisdiction, or any other cause whatsoever. The authority shall always be exercised in the following manner:

- The legislative and executive authority, or lawful agent of and State in controversy with another, shall present a petition to Congress stating the matter in question and asking for a hearing.
- A notice shall be given, by the order of the Congress, to the legislative or executive authority of the other State in the controversy.
- A day will be assigned for the appearance of the parties by their lawful agents who shall then be directed to appoint, by joint

consent, commissioners or judges to constitute a court for hearing and determining the matter in question:

- o If the parties cannot agree, the Congress shall name three persons out of each of the United States, and from the list of such persons each party shall alternately strike out one, the petitioner going first, until the number on the list shall be reduced to thirteen.

- o From that number no less than seven, no more than nine names, as Congress will direct, shall, in the presence of the Congress, be drawn out at random, and the persons whose names are drawn, or any five of them, shall be judges, they will hear and make a final determination to the controversy. The judgment will be made by a yes or no vote of those judges and the majority vote wins.

- o If either party shall neglect to attend on the appointed date and time, without showing reasoning that the Congress judges sufficient, or when present refuse to participate, the Congress will proceed to nominate three persons out of each State, and the Secretary of Congress shall participate on behalf of the party absent or refusing. The judgment and sentence of the court, to be determined in the manner prescribed in this article, shall be final and conclude that issue.

- o If any of the parties refuse to submit to the authority of the court, or to appear to defend their claim or cause, the court will still determine the sentence or judgment. This decision will be final.
- o In order to ensure the security of the parties the judgment or sentence and other proceedings being in either sent to congress, and/or lodged among the acts of Congress, every commissioner, before he sits in judgment shall take an oath. That oath will be administered by one of the judges of the supreme or superior court of the State where the cause shall be tried. The oath shall be, "I will promise to truly hear and determine the matter in question, according to the best of my judgment, without favor, affection, or hope of reward. This is

provided that no State shall be deprived of territory for the benefit of the United States."

All controversies concerning the private ownership of soil claimed under various grants of two or more States, who may hold jurisdiction over these lands, if the boundaries of those States have shifted and those claims are then in question shall be petitioned to the Congress of the United States. Congress will make the final determination as to the true jurisdiction between the different States.

The Congress of the United States shall have the sole and exclusive right and power to:

- Regulate the alloy and value of coin struck under their authority, or by the various States.
- Fixing the standards of weights and measures throughout the United States.
- Regulating the trade and managing all affairs with the Indian tribes, and not members of any of the States. This is provided that the legislative right of any State, within its own boundaries, is not infringed or violated.
- Establishing and regulating post offices from one State to another, throughout the entire United States, as well as charging such postage on the mail passing through

that system as is needed to offset the expenses to this post office.

- Appointing all officers of the land forces in the service of the United States. This is with the exception of the regimental officers.
- Appointing all the officers of the naval forces, and commissioning all officers whatsoever in the services of the United States.
- Make all rules for the governing and regulating of the land and naval forces, and directing their operations.

The Congress of the United States has the authority to appoint a committee, to sit in the recess of the Congress to be named, "A Committee of the States," and to consist of at least one delegate from each State. This committee will appoint other committees and civil officers as may be necessary for managing the general affairs of the United States under their direction with the following provisions:

- To appoint one of their members to preside provided that no person be allowed to service in the Office of the President for more than one year in any term of three years.
- To ascertain the necessary sums of money to be raised for the service of the United States. They sum of money must only be

appropriate and applied for financing the public expenses.

- To borrow money or emit bills on the credit of the United States, communicating every half year to the various States on account of the sums of money borrowed or spent.
- To build and equip a navy.
- To agree upon the number of land forces, and to make requisitions from each State for its quota in proportion to the number of white inhabitants of the various States. The requisition shall be binding.
    - Upon receipt of these quotas each State shall appoint regimental officers, and raise the men.
    - The States will then clothe, arm, and equip these men in a soldier-like manner.
    - All of this will be done at the expense of the United States.
    - Once the officers and men are clothed, armed, and equipped they shall march to the place appointed, and within the agreed upon time by the order of the Congress of the United States.
    - If the Congress of the United States decides that there is special circumstances, they can decide that any State should not raise men, or

should raise a smaller number than its quota. The Congress can also decide that any other State can raise a greater number of men than the original quota.

- o If a State, which has been tasked to raise a greater number of men than the quota, and it decides that the larger number cannot be safely spared, as many men as can be provided safely will be provided.
- o Once the number greater or lower than the quota are raised the officers and men, once clothed, armed and equipped, shall march to the appointed place, by the time agreed upon by the Congress of the United States.

Unless nine out of the States agree to the following items the Congress of the United States shall never:

- Engage in war.
- Grant letters of marque and reprisal in time of peace.
- Enter into any treaties or alliances.
- Coin money or regulate the value of money.
- Establish the sums and expenses necessary for the common defense and welfare of the United States.

- Emit bills.
- Borrow money on the credit of the United States.
- Appropriate money.
- Agree upon the number of vessels of war to be built or purchased.
- Agree upon the number of land or sea forces to be raised.
- Appoint a commander in chief of the army or navy.
- Or any other question except for adjourning from day to day.

The Congress of the United States has the power to adjourn at any time within the year, and to any place within the United States provided that the period of adjournment is no longer than six months. They shall publish the journal of their proceedings on a monthly basis, except for the portions relating to treaties, alliances, or military operations, as in their judgment require secrecy. The yeas and nays of the delegates of each State on any question shall be entered into the Journal, when it is desired by any delegate. The delegates of any State, at his or their request, shall be furnished with a transcript of the Journal except for those parts decided to require secrecy, and those journals can be put before the legislatures of the several States.

Discussion

This section is all about Congressional powers. It tells us, with some reasonable specificity, that the Congress is actually supposed to do. We won't go through them one at a time...that can be seen in the modernized text. There are a few that probably need a bit of explanation, and that is where we will focus, as they are much different that what we would consider necessary to be written into law today.

Most of these powers make sense, for instance Congress has the right to wage war and peace...that makes sense. Under this power, there are two that seem odd.

First is that Congress has the power to decide how War prizes will be divided. One of the ways soldiers were compensated for their services back in this time of our history is that they could plunder the enemy. For instance, if we were fighting a War overseas and soldiers plundered some valuables from the local area they would divide them up amongst themselves. Congress could decide how this took place.

This practice is no longer condoned. In fact, this practice is now punished (and punished harshly) if a soldier does plunder the area in which they operate.

If this practice was still condoned, how do you think a modern Congress would do this?

Would they just keep these war prizes for

themselves?

How would or could they possibly justify this action?

What modern day politician would possibly think that they should be the inheritors of all the wealth possible?

Would they think, "Why should we let those little people keep all those pretty spoils, when the better people would know what to do with them better. Besides its for their own good they don't have to think about problems like money?" Ok a bit of sarcasm there, sorry, we had to get that off our chest.

Second on the War and Peace powers, there is a line that says Congress has the power to grant letters of marque and reprisal. What this translates into is that they can create privateers.

Privateers are not a commonly heard of thing, essentially they are pirates that are hired by various governments. So...sure they are pirates but as long as they work for us they are good guys...kinda. With this being said, Privateers can only use the Letter of Marque against the country in which is stated in the Letter. If they attack and plunder a ship from say Spain, and the letter states that only France can be attacked, the Privateer is just a straight up pirate and subject to all laws and regulations in dealing with them.

The rest of this article is pretty normal stuff. There are some minor bits that are worthy of longer discussion. The final one we wanted to focus on was that the courts will be appointed by the Congress, for the specific purpose of dealing with crimes on the high sea. These courts also get the responsibility for determining what happens to things that are captures on the high seas. So, in other words, if someone captures a ship, or something of value at sea, it is these courts, appointed by the Congress that decided what happens to that item or items of value.

Just like with the spoils of war do you see any potential for corruption there?

Not in the slightest you say, well, we don't see that potential either (should we turn off the sarcasm now?)

Chapter 10

Article X

Original Text to Article X of the Articles of Confederation

The committee of the states, or any nine of them, shall be authorized to execute, in the recess of congress, such of the powers of congress as the united states, in congress assembled, by the consent of nine states, shall, from time to time, think expedient to vest them with; provided that no power be delegated to the said committee, for the exercise of which, by the articles of confederation, the voice of nine states, in the congress of the united states assembled, is requisite.

Modern Text to Article X of the Articles of Confederation

A minimum of nine of the members of the committee of the States is necessary to authorize the execution of powers of the Congress during a recess of that legislative body. The exception to these recess powers are those listed in this document requiring that the full body of the Congress of the United States be assembled.

Discussion

This article sets up what would happen during the times when Congress was in recess. In those cases there would be a committee of States. This group of nine would have the power to do some legislative, bureaucratic, or administrative tasks during the down time.

In reality there were some issues. If you look at the document carefully there is no minimum attendance requirement. The States can have representatives but they have no requirement to show up. There were even some cases where attendance at Congressional meetings was so poor that there were problems holding votes. How do you have a majority vote if you don't have a quorum of the States in attendance? The simple answer is that you cannot.

The attendance at the committee of nine States meetings was often times even worse. No one regarded this group with high regard because they had such limited power. In practice, this committee met only once, in the summer of 1784. It never reached a quorum and was unable to complete any task assigned to it due to such poor attendance.

Besides the poor attendance, does this remind anyone of anything else involving the modern Congress the recent past?

Wouldn't it be nice if we could get the

attendance at the modern Congress so low they couldn't do anything to us?

Might be nice, but the Constitution has attendance requirements and punishments possible if you don't show up. Too bad, we might all be better off if they stopped trying to "improve" our lives. Maybe we could all write them to ask them to stop "improving" our lives so much? Sometimes a little less help would be nice.

Chapter 11

Article XI

Original Text to Article XI of the Articles of Confederation

Canada acceding to this confederation, and joining in the measures of the united states, shall be admitted into, and entitled to all the advantages of this union: but no other colony shall be admitted into the same, unless such admission be agreed to by nine states.

Modern Text to Article XI of the Articles of Confederation

Canada agreeing to this confederation, will be joined to the procedures of the United States shall be admitted into and entitled to all the advantages of this union. No other colony shall be admitted unless such admission is agreed to by a minimum of nine States.

Discussion

This was a very basic article. It didn't say much other than putting into flowery language a simple Statement.

If Canada agrees to everything in this document

they are free to join the confederacy. They were the only colony, other than the original thirteen that was given this right. It is also a little unclear if Canada would be a member State or they would be a colony much like the original thirteen Colonies turned States were to Great Britain.

Interestingly, Canada was a British held colony at the time. Even more interesting, is that Canada turned the offer down for a multitude of reasons. The two main reasons we could uncover were that the people of Canada were tired of war (they had been in low level wars for many years), and, on top of that, they were actually content with British Rule at that point in time.

Now jump forward to today's time, a good debate would be...did Canada make the right decision back then? Hind sight is always 20/20.

Chapter 12

Article XII

Original Text to Article XII of the Articles of Confederation

All bills of credit emitted, monies borrowed, and debts contracted by or under the authority of congress, before the assembling of the united states, in pursuance of the present confederation, shall be deemed and considered as a charge against the United States, for payment and satisfaction whereof the said united states and the public faith are hereby solemnly pledged.

Modern Text to Article XII of the Articles of Confederation

All bills of credit made, money borrowed, and debt contracted under the authority of the Congress before the assembling of the United States, shall be deemed and considered the responsibility of the United States. Payment and satisfaction of these debts are pledged through the public faith and the Congress of the United States.

Discussion

The founders wanted to put into writing that the

debts incurred for the Revolutionary War prior to this document being adopted, would be the responsibility of the Confederacy.

This one is overall pretty simple the founders were honest and honorable men. They wanted to be sure that everyone and every country involved understood they would hold up their end of those debts and not just ignore them.

Plus, if you dig a little deeper, many of the signatories of this document were actually owed money by the government. It was in their best interest to make sure this was well understood.

Chapter 13

Article XIII

Original Text to Article XIII of the Articles of Confederation

Every State shall abide by the determinations of the united states, in congress assembled, on all questions which by this confederation are submitted to them. And the Articles of this confederation shall be inviolably observed by every state, and the union shall be perpetual; nor shall any alteration at any time hereafter be made in any of them, unless such alteration be agreed to in a congress of the united states, and be afterwards con-firmed by the legislatures of every state.

And Whereas it hath pleased the Great Governor of the World to incline the hearts of the legislatures we respectively represent in congress, to approve of, and to authorize us to ratify the said articles of confederation and perpetual union, Know Ye, that we, the undersigned delegates, by virtue of the power and authority to us given for that purpose, do, by these presents, in the name and in behalf of our respective constituents, fully and entirely ratify and confirm each and every of the said articles of confederation and perpetual union, and all and singular the matters and things therein contained. And we do further solemnly plight and engage the faith of our respective constituents, that they shall abide by the determinations of the united states in congress assembled, on all questions, which by the said confederation are submitted to them. And that the articles thereof shall be inviolably observed by the states we respectively represent, and that the union shall be perpetual. In Witness whereof, we have hereunto set our hands, in Congress. Done at Philadelphia, in the State of Pennsylvania, the ninth Day of July, in the Year of our Lord one Thousand seven Hundred and Seventy eight, and in the third year of the Independence of America.

Modern Text to Article XIII of the Articles of Confederation

Every State shall accept the determinations of the Congress of the United States on all questions submitted to them by this Confederation. These Articles of Confederation shall be inviolably observed by every State and this Union shall be everlasting. No alteration at any time henceforth will be made to any of them unless such alteration is agreed to in the Congress of the United States and afterwards confirmed by the legislatures of every States.

Whereas it has pleased the Lord to incline the hearts of the legislatures we represent in this Congress, to approve of, and to authorize us to ratify these Articles of Confederation and perpetual union. We the undersigned delegates, by the virtue of the power and authority given to us for that purpose, do by these signatures, in the name and on behalf of our constituents, fully and entirely ratify and confirm each and every Article of the Confederation and perpetual union and all things contained therein. We solemnly swear with the faith of our respective constituents, that they shall abide by the determinations of the Congress of the United States, on all questions submitted to the Confederation. These articles shall be inviolably observed be the States we represent and the union formed shall be perpetual. In witness thereof, we have signed our names, in Congress. We have done this in the city of Philadelphia in the State of Pennsylvania, on the ninth day of July, in the Year of our Lord one thousand seven hundred and seventy eight, in the third year of the Independence of America.

Discussion

This article says that this document, and this union of States are perpetual.

It also says that these articles can be modified, as in the future there will probably be some change necessary. Think of it like an amendment process for the Articles of Confederation. In the Constitution there are specific mechanisms for passing amendments involving a supermajority of votes to the affirmative. The Articles, on the other hand, would only allow amendments with a unanimous vote. Once again thinking back to a previous statement, how often do you think a middle to large size group of men could get together and totally agree on any issue or item.

In our humble opinions, something like that would not happen often if even at all.

Chapter 14

The Original Presidents of the United States

Introduction

It is not widely thought about, or even discussed, that the United States had presidents prior to George Washington. They all served under The Articles of Confederation. President Washington was our first Constitutional President. He deserves our great respect and was a fantastic leader but we want to discuss a little bit, maybe a paragraph or two, about each of these other men. There could easily be a book length work on any of them (and on some this already exists).

John Hanson 1782

President Hanson was a merchant as well as a public officeholder from Maryland. He was also a signer to the Articles of Confederation having been sent by Maryland as one of the delegates.

His life in public office began in 1750 when he served as a Sheriff in Charles County Maryland. He went on to be elected to represent that county in the lower house of the Maryland General Assembly. His career culminated in his being elected as the very first President of the United States. He served just one term and died in November of 1783. His career and life deserves far more than the two paragraphs we have here but he was a patriot and served the country whenever asked.

Elias Boudinot 1783

President Boudinot was a lawyer (no one is perfect) from New Jersey. He had a long and distinguished career in public office. He was one of the original delegates that signed the Articles of Confederation and served as the second President.

He focused his efforts on leadership of the young Nation throughout the Revolutionary War. Following the War he was elected as a Congressmen from New Jersey under the Constitution. His final public office was as the director of the US Mint, an office George Washington appointed him to and he served in that role from 1795 to 1805.

Thomas Mifflin 1784

President Mifflin was truly one of the founding fathers. The man was everywhere. He served in many different public offices and retired with distinction. His complete list of offices held, besides being a President under the Articles of

Confederation, includes: A Major General in the Continental Army, twice the Quartermaster General during the Revolution, a member of the Pennsylvania Provincial Assembly, A Continental Congressman from Pennsylvania, President of the Continental Congress, a delegate to the Constitutional Convention, Speaker of the Pennsylvania House of Representatives, President of the Pennsylvania Supreme Executive Council, and he was the very first Governor of the State of Pennsylvania. Ok, we think we got it all.

If you visit Pennsylvania you can see his grave (he died in the year 1800), and is buried in front of Trinity Church in Lancaster.

Richard Henry Lee 1785

He was an American elected official from Virginia. He was the man that in the second Continental Congress called for the colonies to declare their independence from Great Britain. His resolution led directly to the Declaration of Independence being written and eventually signed. He was also a signatory to the Articles of Confederation. Once the Constitution was in ratified he was elected as a Senator from his home State of Virginia and during part of his time in that office (1789-1792) he served as the President pro tempore of the Senate.

John Hancock 1786

John Hancock is a man who really needs no introduction. He was a merchant, a statement and a very prominent member of the founding fathers. He was, among other things, the first and third Governor of the Commonwealth of Massachusetts. Prior to the Revolutionary War Mr. Hancock was one of the wealthiest men in the Thirteen Colonies. He started his career in Boston and learned his Statesmanship from Sam Adams (it is unknown of they drank beer together).

We could go on about him for many, many pages. However, this book is not intended to be anything more than introductory. However, if you look at a picture of the Declaration of Independence you will see his signature prominently displayed and written very largely. He wanted to be sure King George could see his name without his glasses. He was that resolute about the Colonies being independent. Lucky for us he got his wish or we would all be drinking tea instead of Mocha Lattes.

Nation Gorman 1787

He was only President for about six months, but deserves our respect. He was a merchant from Massachusetts and a delegate to the Continental Congress. He was a signer of the U.S. Constitution and while not one of the more prolific of the founding fathers did his part for the Revolution whenever he was called upon.

Arthur Saint Clair 1788

He was a soldier as well as a politician. Interestingly he served in the British Army during the French and Indian War before moving to Pennsylvania. Throughout the Revolutionary War he achieved the rank of Major General (2 stars), but was eventually removed from a command position after he retreated during a key battle. He left the military and became a full time politician and continued to serve the new Nation.

Cyrus Griffin 1789

He was a lawyer as well as a judge who served as the last President of the Continental Congress. He resigned his position once the current U.S. Constitution was ratified. He left elected office and was appointed as a federal judge.

Chapter 15

The Original Texas of the Articles of Confederation

Introduction

To all to whom these Presents shall come, we, the undersigned Delegates of the States affixed to our Names send greeting. Whereas the Delegates of the United States of America in Congress assembled did on the fifteenth day of November in the year of our Lord One Thousand Seven Hundred and Seventy seven, and in the Second Year of the Independence of America agree to certain articles of Confederation and perpetual Union between the States of New Hampshire, Massachusetts-bay, Rhode Island and Providence Plantations, Connecticut, New York, New Jersey, Pennsylvania, Delaware, Maryland, Virginia, North Carolina, South Carolina, and Georgia in the Words following, viz. "Articles of Confederation and perpetual Union between the States of New Hampshire, Massachusetts-bay, Rhode Island and Providence Plantations, Connecticut, New York, New Jersey,

Pennsylvania, Delaware, Maryland, Virginia, North Carolina, South Carolina, and Georgia.

Article I

The Stile of this confederacy shall be, "The United States of America."

Article II

Each state retains its sovereignty, freedom and independence, and every Power, Jurisdiction and right, which is not by this confederation expressly delegated to the United States, in Congress assembled.

Article III

The said states hereby severally enter into a firm league of friendship with each other, for their common defence, the security of their Liberties, and their mutual and general welfare, binding themselves to assist each other, against all force offered to, or attacks made upon them, or any of them, on account of religion, sovereignty, trade, or any other pretence whatever.

Article IV

The better to secure and perpetuate mutual friendship and intercourse among the people of the different states in this union, the free inhabitants of each of these states, paupers, vagabonds and fugitives from Justice excepted, shall be entitled to all privileges and immunities of free citizens in the several states; and the people of each state shall have free ingress and regress to and from any other state, and shall enjoy therein all the privileges of trade and commerce, subject to the same duties, impositions and restrictions as the inhabitants thereof respectively, provided that such restrictions shall not extend so far as to prevent the removal of property imported into any state, to any other State of which the Owner is an inhabitant; provided also that no imposition, duties or restriction shall be laid by any state, on the property of the united states, or either of them.

If any Person guilty of, or charged with, treason, felony, or other high misdemeanor in any state, shall flee from Justice, and be found in any of the united states, he shall upon demand of the Governor or executive power of the state from which he fled, be delivered up, and removed to the state having jurisdiction of his offence.

Full faith and credit shall be given in each of these states to the records, acts and judicial proceedings of the courts and magistrates of every other state.

Article V

For the more convenient management of the general interests of the united states, delegates shall be annually appointed in such manner as the legislature of each state shall direct, to meet in Congress on the first Monday in November, in every year, with a power reserved to each state to recall its delegates, or any of them, at any time within the year, and to send others in their stead, for the remainder of the Year.

No State shall be represented in Congress by less than two, nor by more than seven Members; and no person shall be capable of being delegate for more than three years, in any term of six years; nor shall any person, being a delegate, be capable of holding any office under the united states, for which he, or another for his benefit receives any salary, fees or emolument of any kind.

Each State shall maintain its own delegates in a meeting of the states, and while they act as members of the committee of the states.

In determining questions in the United States, in Congress assembled, each state shall have one vote.

Freedom of speech and debate in Congress shall not be impeached or questioned in any Court, or place out of Congress, and the members of congress shall be protected in their persons from arrests and imprisonments, during the time of their going to and from, and attendance on congress, except for treason, felony, or breach of the peace.

Article VI

No State, without the Consent of the united States, in congress assembled, shall send any embassy to, or receive any embassy from, or enter into any conferrence, agreement, alliance, or treaty, with any King prince or state; nor shall any person holding any office of profit or trust under the united states, or any of them, accept of any present, emolument, office, or title of any kind whatever, from any king, prince, or foreign state; nor shall the united states, in congress assembled, or any of them, grant any title of nobility.

No two or more states shall enter into any treaty,

confederation, or alliance whatever between them, without the consent of the united states, in congress assembled, specifying accurately the purposes for which the same is to be entered into, and how long it shall continue.

No State shall lay any imposts or duties, which may interfere with any stipulations in treaties, entered into by the united States in congress assembled, with any king, prince, or State, in pursuance of any treaties already proposed by congress, to the courts of France and Spain.

No vessels of war shall be kept up in time of peace, by any state, except such number only, as shall be deemed necessary by the united states, in congress assembled, for the defence of such state, or its trade; nor shall any body of forces be kept up, by any state, in time of peace, except such number only as, in the judgment of the united states, in congress assembled, shall be deemed requisite to garrison the forts necessary for the defence of such state; but every state shall always keep up a well regulated and disciplined militia, sufficiently armed and accounted, and shall provide and constantly have ready for use, in public stores, a due number of field pieces and tents, and a proper quantity of arms, ammunition, and camp equipage.

No State shall engage in any war without the consent of the united States in congress assembled, unless such State be actually invaded by enemies, or shall have received certain advice of a resolution being formed by some nation of Indians to invade such State, and the danger is so imminent as not to admit of a delay till the united states in congress assembled, can be consulted: nor shall any state grant commissions to any ships or vessels of war, nor letters of marque or reprisal, except it be after a declaration of war by the united states in congress assembled, and then only against the kingdom or State, and the subjects thereof, against which war has been so declared, and under such regulations as shall be established by the united states in congress assembled, unless such state be infested by pirates, in which case vessels of war may be fitted out for that occasion, and kept so long as the danger shall continue, or until the united states in congress assembled shall determine otherwise.

Article VII

When land forces are raised by any state, for the common defence, all officers of or under the rank of colonel, shall be appointed by the legislature of each state respectively by whom such forces shall be raised, or in such manner as such state shall direct, and all vacancies shall be filled up by the state which first made appointment.

Article VIII

All charges of war, and all other expenses that shall be incurred for the common defence or general welfare, and allowed by the united states in congress assembled, shall be defrayed out of a common treasury, which shall be supplied by the several states, in proportion to the value of all land within each state, granted to or surveyed for any Person, as such land and the buildings and improvements thereon shall be estimated, according to such mode as the united states, in congress assembled, shall, from time to time, direct and appoint. The taxes for paying that proportion shall be laid and levied by the authority and direction of the legislatures of the several states within the time agreed upon by the United States in congress assembled.

Article IX

The United States, in congress assembled, shall have the sole and exclusive right and power of determining on peace and war, except in the cases mentioned in the sixth article - of sending and receiving ambassadors - entering into treaties and alliances, provided that no treaty of commerce shall be made, whereby the legislative power of the respective states shall be restrained from imposing such imposts and duties on foreigners, as their own people are subjected to, or from prohibiting the exportation or importation of any species of goods or commodities whatsoever - of establishing rules for deciding, in all cases, what captures on land or water shall be legal, and in what manner prizes taken by land or naval forces in the service of the united Sates, shall be divided or appropriated - of granting letters of marque and reprisal in times of peace - appointing courts for the trial of piracies and felonies committed on the high seas; and establishing courts; for receiving and determining finally appeals in all cases of captures; provided that no member of congress shall be appointed a judge of any of the said courts.

The united states, in congress assembled, shall also be the last resort on appeal, in all disputes and differences now subsisting, or that hereafter may arise between two or more states concerning boundary, jurisdiction, or any other cause whatever; which authority shall always be exercised in the manner following. Whenever the legislative or executive authority, or lawful agent of any state in controversy with another, shall present a petition to congress, stating the matter in question, and praying for a hearing, notice thereof shall be given, by order of congress, to the legislative or executive authority of the other state in controversy, and a day assigned for the appearance of the parties by their lawful agents, who shall then be directed to appoint, by joint consent, commissioners or judges to constitute a court for hearing and determining the matter in question: but if they cannot agree, congress shall name three persons out of each of the united states, and from the list of such persons each party shall alternately strike out one, the petitioners beginning, until the number shall be reduced to thirteen; and from that number not less than seven, nor more than nine names, as congress shall direct, shall, in the presence of congress, be drawn out by lot, and the persons whose names shall be so drawn, or any five of them, shall be commissioners or judges, to hear and finally determine the controversy, so always as a major part of the judges, who shall hear the cause, shall agree in the determination: and if either party shall neglect to attend at the day appointed, without showing reasons which congress shall judge sufficient, or being present, shall refuse to strike, the congress shall proceed to nominate three persons out of each State, and the secretary of congress shall strike in behalf of such party absent or refusing; and the judgment and sentence of the court, to be appointed in the manner before prescribed, shall be final and conclusive; and if any of the parties shall refuse to submit to the authority of such court, or to appear or defend their claim or cause, the court shall nevertheless proceed to pronounce sentence, or judgment, which shall in like manner be final and decisive; the judgment or sentence and other proceedings being in either case transmitted to congress, and lodged among the acts of congress, for the security of the parties concerned: provided that every commissioner, before he sits in judgment, shall take an oath to be administered by one of the judges of the supreme or superior court of the State where the cause shall be tried, "well and truly to hear and determine the matter in question, according to the best of his judgment, without favour, affection, or hope of reward: "provided, also, that no State shall be deprived of territory for the benefit of the united states.

All controversies concerning the private right of soil claimed under different grants of two or more states, whose jurisdictions as they may respect such lands, and the states which passed such grants are adjusted, the said grants or either of them being at the same time claimed to have originated antecedent to such settlement of jurisdiction, shall, on the petition of either party to the congress of the united states, be finally determined, as near as may be, in the same manner as is before prescribed for deciding disputes respecting territorial jurisdiction between different states.

The united states, in congress assembled, shall also have the sole and exclusive right and power of regulating the alloy and value of coin struck by their own authority, or by that of the respective states - fixing the standard of weights and measures throughout the united states - regulating the trade and managing all affairs with the Indians, not members of any of the states; provided that the legislative right of any state, within its own limits, be not infringed or violated - establishing and regulating post-offices from one state to another, throughout all the united states, and exacting such postage on the papers passing through the same, as may be requisite to defray the expenses of the said office - appointing all officers of the land forces in the service of the united States, excepting regimental officers - appointing all the officers of the naval forces, and commissioning all officers whatever in the service of the united states; making rules for the government and regulation of the said land and naval forces, and directing their operations.

The united States, in congress assembled, shall have authority to appoint a committee, to sit in the recess of congress, to be denominated, "A Committee of the States," and to consist of one delegate from each State; and to appoint such other committees and civil officers as may be necessary for managing the general affairs of the united states under their direction - to appoint one of their number to preside; provided that no person be allowed to serve in the office of president more than one year in any term of three years; to ascertain the necessary sums of money to be raised for the service of the united states, and to appropriate and apply the same for defraying the public expenses; to borrow money or emit bills on the credit of the united states, transmitting every half year to the respective states an account of the sums of money so borrowed or emitted, - to build and equip a navy - to agree upon the number of land forces, and to make requisitions from each state for its quota, in proportion to the number of white inhabitants in such state, which requisition shall be binding; and thereupon the legislature of each state shall appoint the regimental officers, raise the men, and clothe, arm, and equip them, in a soldier-like manner, at the expense of the united states; and the officers and men so clothed, armed, and equipped, shall march to the place appointed, and within the time agreed on by the united states, in congress assembled; but if the united states, in congress assembled, shall, on consideration of circumstances, judge proper that any state should not raise men, or should raise a smaller number than its quota, and that any other state should raise a greater number of men than the quota thereof, such extra number shall be raised, officered, clothed, armed, and equipped in the same manner as the quota of such state, unless the legislature of such state shall judge that such extra number cannot be safely spared out of the same, in which case they shall raise, officer, clothe, arm, and equip, as many of such extra number as they judge can be safely spared. And the officers and men so clothed, armed, and equipped, shall march to the place appointed, and within the time agreed on by the united states in congress assembled.

The united states, in congress assembled, shall never engage in a war, nor grant letters of marque and reprisal in time of peace, nor enter into any treaties or alliances, nor coin money, nor regulate the value thereof nor ascertain the sums and expenses necessary for the defence and welfare of the united states, or any of them, nor emit bills, nor borrow money on the credit of the united states, nor appropriate money, nor agree upon the number of vessels of war to be built or purchased, or the number of land or sea forces to be raised, nor appoint a commander in chief of the army or navy, unless nine states assent to the same, nor shall a question on any other point, except for adjourning from day to day, be determined, unless by the votes of a majority of the united states in congress assembled.

The congress of the united states shall have power to adjourn to any time within the year, and to any place within the united states, so that no period of adjournment be for a longer duration than the space of six Months, and shall publish the Journal of their proceedings monthly, except such parts thereof relating to treaties, alliances, or military operations, as in their judgment require secrecy; and the yeas and nays of the delegates of each State, on any question, shall be entered on the Journal, when it is desired by any delegate; and the delegates of a State, or any of them, at his or their request, shall be furnished with a transcript of the said Journal, except such parts as are above excepted, to lay before the legislatures of the several states.

Article X

The committee of the states, or any nine of them, shall be authorized to execute, in the recess of congress, such of the powers of congress as the united states, in congress assembled, by the consent of nine states, shall, from time to time, think expedient to vest them with; provided that no power be delegated to the said committee, for the exercise of which, by the articles of confederation, the voice of nine states, in the congress of the united states assembled, is requisite.

Article XI

Canada acceding to this confederation, and joining in the measures of the united states, shall be admitted into, and entitled to all the advantages of this union: but no other colony shall be admitted into the same, unless such admission be agreed to by nine states.

Article XII

All bills of credit emitted, monies borrowed, and debts contracted by or under the authority of congress, before the assembling of the united states, in pursuance of the present confederation, shall be deemed and considered as a charge against the United States, for payment and satisfaction whereof the said united states and the public faith are hereby solemnly pledged.

Article XIII

Every State shall abide by the determinations of

the united states, in congress assembled, on all questions which by this confederation are submitted to them. And the Articles of this confederation shall be inviolably observed by every state, and the union shall be perpetual; nor shall any alteration at any time hereafter be made in any of them, unless such alteration be agreed to in a congress of the united states, and be afterwards con-firmed by the legislatures of every state.

And Whereas it hath pleased the Great Governor of the World to incline the hearts of the legislatures we respectively represent in congress, to approve of, and to authorize us to ratify the said articles of confederation and perpetual union, Know Ye, that we, the undersigned delegates, by virtue of the power and authority to us given for that purpose, do, by these presents, in the name and in behalf of our respective constituents, fully and entirely ratify and confirm each and every of the said articles of confederation and perpetual union, and all and singular the matters and things therein contained. And we do further solemnly plight and engage the faith of our respective constituents, that they shall abide by the determinations of the united states in congress assembled, on all questions, which by the said confederation are submitted to them. And that the articles thereof shall be inviolably observed by the states we respectively represent, and that the union shall be perpetual. In Witness whereof, we have hereunto set our hands, in Congress. Done at Philadelphia, in the State of Pennsylvania, the ninth Day of July, in the Year of our Lord one Thousand seven Hundred and Seventy eight, and in the third year of the Independence of America.

Chapter 16

The Modernized Text of the Articles of Confederation

Introduction

To all those who read this document, we, the signers who are all delegates of the various States send greetings. This is done while the representatives of the United States of America assembled on the fifteenth day of November in the year of our Lord one thousand seven hundred and seventy seven. This was in the second year of the Independent American State and we agree upon these Articles of Confederation.

These Articles will ensure a perpetual union between the States of New Hampshire, Massachusetts Bay, Rhode Island and Providence Plantations, Connecticut, New York, New Jersey, Pennsylvania, Delaware, Maryland, Virginia, North Carolina, South Carolina and Georgia. This document represents those agreed upon Articles and will be the governing principals of this Nation.

Article I

The name of this confederacy shall be, "The United States of America."

Article II

Each state will retain its own sovereignty, freedom, and independence. The independent States retain every power, jurisdiction and right, which is not expressly delegated to the United States.

Article III

The several States are hereby entered into a firm alliance of friendship with one another. This will allow them to provide for their common defense, secure their liberties, and provide for the mutual and general welfare. This alliance binds them together to assist one another against external force or attacks made on their territories. This is no matter if those attacks are made on account of religion, sovereignty, trade, or any other reasons whatsoever.

Article IV

To better ensure and perpetuate the mutual friendship as well as interaction among the people of the various States in the union, the free inhabitants of each State, with the exception of fugitives from justice, shall be entitled to all privileges and immunities of free citizens. The people of each State shall have free entry and return to, and from, any other State. The citizens of each State shall enjoy all the privileges of trade and commerce subject to the same duties, obligations, and restrictions of residents of each respective State, provided that such restrictions do not prevent the removal of property important to any State of which the owner is a resident. No State shall place an obligation, duty or restriction on the property of the United States or any of the other States of this union.

If a person is guilty of, or charged with, treason, felony, or other high misdemeanor in any State, then flees from justice, and is found to be in any of the other States of this Union, they shall be returned to the State in which the offense took place upon request of the Governor or executive of that original State.

Records, acts, and judicial proceedings of the courts and judges considered valid in one State shall be considered valid, as well as given full faith and credit, in every other State.

Article V

In order to better manage the general interests of the United States, delegates shall be appointed on an annual basis in a method determined by the legislature of each State. These delegates will meet in Congress on the first Monday in November, every year. Each State reserves the power to recall some or all of its delegates at any time, for any reason, within the year. If a State recalls its delegates that State must send replacement delegates for the remainder of the year.

No State shall have less than two or more than seven members in the Congress at any one time. No person from a State elected to the Congress shall be a delegate for more than three years inside a six-year time period. No person who is a delegate will hold an office under the United States in which he or she, or someone else for his or her benefit, receives any kind of salary, fee or payment of any kind.

Each State shall pay for their own delegates while they are in a meeting of the States, and while they act as members of the Committee of the States.

In determining questions posed to the United States, in the assembled Congress, each State shall have one vote without regard to the number of delegates.

Freedom of speech and debate in Congress will not be prosecuted or questioned in any Court, or any other place outside of Congress. The members of Congress shall be protected from arrest or imprisonment while they are going to, from, or attending Congress with the exception of treason, felony, or breach of peace.

Article VI

No State, without the consent of the Congress of the United States, shall send a delegation to, receive a delegation from, or enter into a discussion, agreement, alliance, or treaty with any king, prince or foreign state. No person holding a salaried office or position of trust under the United States, or any of the States of the union, may accept any present, payment, office, or title of any kind from a king, prince, or foreign state.

The Congress of the United States will not grant any title of nobility.

No two or more States shall enter into a treaty, coalition, or alliance between themselves, without the consent of the Congress of the United States. The States wishing to do so must accurately specify the purpose for which the proposed treaty, coalition, or alliance is being formed, and how long it is to continue.

No State shall put in place any taxes or duties, which may interfere with any of the stipulations in treaties to which the Congress of the United States has become a signatory. These include any treaties, existing or future, with a king, prince, or foreign state, including those already proposed by Congress to the courts of France and Spain.

No vessels intended for use in war shall be kept in time of peace, by any of the member States, except in such quantity as shall be deemed necessary by the Congress of the United States. This quantity will be the number deemed necessary for defense of the States and their trade. No group of forces shall be kept by any State in time of peace, except in the quantity judged necessary by the Congress of the United States to garrison the forts necessary for defensive purposes. Each State shall keep a well-regulated and disciplined militia, sufficiently armed. Each State shall provide and keep ready for use, in public storage, field equipment, tents, and a proper quantity of arms and ammunition to equip their militia.

No State shall engage in any war without the consent of the Congress of the United States unless that State has been invaded by enemy forces or unless that State has received a resolution being formed by some Nation of Indians to invade the State, and the danger is so imminent that delay of defense until the Congress of the United States can be assembled and consulted.

No State shall grant commissions to any ships or vessels of war, nor letters of reprisal, except after a declaration of war by the Congress of the United States. Once that declaration of war has been made, the States may only perform these tasks against the enemy that is the subject of the declaration of war. These will only be done by the States under regulations as shall be established by the Congress of the United States, unless the State is infested by pirates. In that case vessels of war may be fitted for the occasions, and kept only long as long as the danger exists, or until the Congress of the United States can assemble and determine otherwise.

Article VII

When a land force (Army) is raised by any State in order to provide for the common defense, all officers under the rank of Colonel will be appointed by the legislature of that State. If the State writes a law that dictates a different method then it is that State's law which will determine the method by which these officers are appointed. All vacancies amongst the officer corps shall be filled by the State that first made the appointment. The Congress shall appoint officers with ranks higher than Colonel.

Article VIII

If the Congress of the United States directs costs as a result of war or other expenses resulting from the common defense or general welfare, these costs shall be paid from a common treasury. The treasury shall be supplied by the several States.

The portion of that treasury that comes from each State is in proportion to the value of all land within each State, with the value of buildings and improvements to be estimated. These values shall be determined in a method determined by the Congress of the United States. The taxes for paying that portion of the treasure that is the responsibility of each of the several States are due within the time agreed upon by the Congress of the United States.

Article IX

The Congress of the United States shall have the sole and exclusive right and power of determining the following issues:

- Determining peace and war, except in those cases mentioned in the sixth article.
- Of sending and receiving ambassadors.
- Of entering into treaties and alliances, provided that no treaty of commerce shall be made. The legislative power of the several States shall be restrained from imposing taxes and duties on foreigners, as their own citizens are subjected to, or from prohibiting the exporting or importing of any type of goods or commodities whatsoever.
- The following issues involving legalities:
  - Of establishing rules for deciding, in all cases, which captures on land or water are legal, and in what way prizes are taking by land or naval forces in the services of the United States will be divided amongst the soldiers and sailors.
  - Of granting letters of marque and reprisal in peacetime.
  - Of appointing judges to courts for the trial of piracies and felonies committed on the high seas.
  - Of establishing courts.

- For receiving and determining final appeals in all cases of captures.
- No member of the Congress shall be appointed to be a judge of any of the courts or court related issues.

The Congress of the United States shall be the appeal of last resort, in all disputes and differences now subsisting, or that may arise after this date between two or more States concerning boundaries, jurisdiction, or any other cause whatsoever. The authority shall always be exercised in the following manner:

- The legislative and executive authority, or lawful agent of and State in controversy with another, shall present a petition to Congress stating the matter in question and asking for a hearing.
- A notice shall be given, by the order of the Congress, to the legislative or executive authority of the other State in the controversy.
- A day will be assigned for the appearance of the parties by their lawful agents who shall then be directed to appoint, by joint consent, commissioners or judges to constitute a court for hearing and determining the matter in question:

- If the parties cannot agree, the Congress shall name three persons out of each of the United States, and from the list of such persons each party shall alternately strike out one, the petitioner going first, until the number on the list shall be reduced to thirteen.

- From that number no less than seven, no more than nine names, as Congress will direct, shall, in the presence of the Congress, be drawn out at random, and the persons whose names are drawn, or any five of them, shall be judges, they will hear and make a final determination to the controversy. The judgment will be made by a yes or no vote of those judges and the majority vote wins.

- If either party shall neglect to attend on the appointed date and time, without showing reasoning that the Congress judges sufficient, or when present refuse to participate, the Congress will proceed to nominate three persons out of each State, and the Secretary of Congress shall participate on behalf of the party absent or refusing. The judgment and sentence of the court, to be determined in the manner prescribed in this article, shall be final and conclude that issue.

o If any of the parties refuse to submit to the authority of the court, or to appear to defend their claim or cause, the court will still determine the sentence or judgment. This decision will be final.

o In order to ensure the security of the parties the judgment or sentence and other proceedings being in either sent to congress, and/or lodged among the acts of Congress, every commissioner, before he sits in judgment shall take an oath. That oath will be administered by one of the judges of the supreme or superior court of the State where the cause shall be tried. The oath shall be, "I will promise to truly hear and determine the matter in question, according to the best of my judgment, without favor, affection, or hope of reward. This is provided that no State shall be deprived of territory for the benefit of the United States."

All controversies concerning the private ownership of soil claimed under various grants of two or more States, who may hold jurisdiction over these lands, if the boundaries of those States have shifted and those claims are then in question shall be petitioned to the Congress of the United States. Congress will make the final determination as to the true jurisdiction between the different States.

The Congress of the United States shall have the sole and exclusive right and power to:

- Regulate the alloy and value of coin struck under their authority, or by the various States.
- Fixing the standards of weights and measures throughout the United States.
- Regulating the trade and managing all affairs with the Indian tribes, and not members of any of the States. This is provided that the legislative right of any State, within its own boundaries, is not infringed or violated.
- Establishing and regulating post offices from one State to another, throughout the entire United States, as well as charging such postage on the mail passing through that system as is needed to offset the expenses to this post office.
- Appointing all officers of the land forces in the service of the United States. This is

with the exception of the regimental officers.

- Appointing all the officers of the naval forces, and commissioning all officers whatsoever in the services of the United States.
- Make all rules for the governing and regulating of the land and naval forces, and directing their operations.

The Congress of the United States has the authority to appoint a committee, to sit in the recess of the Congress to be named, "A Committee of the States," and to consist of at least one delegate from each State. This committee will appoint other committees and civil officers as may be necessary for managing the general affairs of the United States under their direction with the following provisions:

- To appoint one of their members to preside provided that no person be allowed to service in the Office of the President for more than one year in any term of three years.
- To ascertain the necessary sums of money to be raised for the service of the United States. They sum of money must only be appropriate and applied for financing the public expenses.
- To borrow money or emit bills on the credit of the United States,

communicating every half year to the various States on account of the sums of money borrowed or spent.

- To build and equip a navy.
- To agree upon the number of land forces, and to make requisitions from each State for its quota in proportion to the number of white inhabitants of the various States. The requisition shall be binding.
  - Upon receipt of these quotas each State shall appoint regimental officers, and raise the men.
  - The States will then clothe, arm, and equip these men in a soldier-like manner.
  - All of this will be done at the expense of the United States.
  - Once the officers and men are clothed, armed, and equipped they shall march to the place appointed, and within the agreed upon time by the order of the Congress of the United States.
  - If the Congress of the United States decides that there is special circumstances, they can decide that any State should not raise men, or should raise a smaller number than its quota. The Congress can also decide that any other State can

raise a greater number of men than the original quota.

o If a State, which has been tasked to raise a greater number of men than the quota, and it decides that the larger number cannot be safely spared, as many men as can be provided safely will be provided.

o Once the number greater or lower than the quota are raised the officers and men, once clothed, armed and equipped, shall march to the appointed place, by the time agreed upon by the Congress of the United States.

Unless nine out of the States agree to the following items the Congress of the United States shall never:

- Engage in war.
- Grant letters of marque and reprisal in time of peace.
- Enter into any treaties or alliances.
- Coin money or regulate the value of money.
- Establish the sums and expenses necessary for the common defense and welfare of the United States.
- Emit bills.
- Borrow money on the credit of the United States.

- Appropriate money.
- Agree upon the number of vessels of war to be built or purchased.
- Agree upon the number of land or sea forces to be raised.
- Appoint a commander in chief of the army or navy.
- Or any other question except for adjourning from day to day.

The Congress of the United States has the power to adjourn at any time within the year, and to any place within the United States provided that the period of adjournment is no longer than six months. They shall publish the journal of their proceedings on a monthly basis, except for the portions relating to treaties, alliances, or military operations, as in their judgment require secrecy. The yeas and nays of the delegates of each State on any question shall be entered into the Journal, when it is desired by any delegate. The delegates of any State, at his or their request, shall be furnished with a transcript of the Journal except for those parts decided to require secrecy, and those journals can be put before the legislatures of the several States.

Article X

A minimum of nine of the members of the

committee of the States is necessary to authorize the execution of powers of the Congress during a recess of that legislative body. The exception to these recess powers are those listed in this document requiring that the full body of the Congress of the United States be assembled.

Article XI

Canada agreeing to this confederation, will be joined to the procedures of the United States shall be admitted into and entitled to all the advantages of this union. No other colony shall be admitted unless such admission is agreed to by a minimum of nine States.

Article XII

All bills of credit made, money borrowed, and debt contracted under the authority of the Congress before the assembling of the United States, shall be deemed and considered the responsibility of the United States. Payment and satisfaction of these debts are pledged through the public faith and the Congress of the United States.

Article XIII

Every State shall accept the determinations of the Congress of the United States on all questions submitted to them by this Confederation. These Articles of Confederation shall be inviolably observed by every State and this Union shall be everlasting. No alteration at any time henceforth will be made to any of them unless such alteration is agreed to in the Congress of the United States and afterwards confirmed by the legislatures of every States.

Whereas it has pleased the Lord to incline the hearts of the legislatures we represent in this Congress, to approve of, and to authorize us to ratify these Articles of Confederation and perpetual union. We the undersigned delegates, by the virtue of the power and authority given to us for that purpose, do by these signatures, in the name and on behalf of our constituents, fully and entirely ratify and confirm each and every Article of the Confederation and perpetual union and all things contained therein. We solemnly swear with the faith of our respective constituents, that they shall abide by the determinations of the Congress of the United States, on all questions submitted to the Confederation. These articles shall be inviolably observed be the States we represent and the union formed shall be perpetual. In witness thereof, we have signed our names, in Congress. We have done this in the city of Philadelphia in the State of Pennsylvania, on the ninth day of July, in the Year of our Lord one thousand seven hundred and seventy eight, in the third year of the Independence of America.